D1709701

Food Dudes

S. TRUETT CATHY

Chick-fil-A Founder

Heather C. Hudak

Checkerboard
Library

An Imprint of Abdo Publishing
www.abdopublishing.com

abdopublishing.com

Published by Abdo Publishing, a division of ABDO, PO Box 398166, Minneapolis, Minnesota 55439. Copyright © 2018 by Abdo Consulting Group, Inc. International copyrights reserved in all countries. No part of this book may be reproduced in any form without written permission from the publisher. Checkerboard Library™ is a trademark and logo of Abdo Publishing.

Printed in the United States of America, North Mankato, Minnesota
062017
092017

THIS BOOK CONTAINS
RECYCLED MATERIALS

Production: Mighty Media, Inc.
Editor: Rebecca Felix
Cover Photographs: AP Images (inset), Mighty Media, Inc. (main)
Interior Photographs: Alamy, pp. 9, 13, 17; AP Images, pp. 1, 21; Chick-fil-A, p. 11; Clinton Steeds/Flickr, p. 15; Shutterstock, pp. 5, 7, 12, 19, 25, 27; WinShape Camps, p. 23

Publisher's Cataloging-in-Publication Data

Names: Hudak, Heather C., 1975-, author.
Title: S. Truett Cathy: Chick-Fil-A founder / by Heather C. Hudak.
Other titles: Chick-Fil-A founder
Description: Minneapolis, MN : Abdo Publishing, 2018. | Series: Food dudes |
    Includes bibliographical references and index.
Identifiers: LCCN 2016962854 | ISBN 9781532110801 (lib. bdg.) |
    ISBN 9781680788655 (ebook)
Subjects: LCSH: Cathy, S. Truett, 1921-2014--Juvenile literature. | Chick-Fil-A
    (Firm)--United States--Biography--Juvenile literature. | Restaurateurs--United
    States--Biography--Juvenile literature. | Businesspeople--United States--
    Biography--Juvenile literature.
Classification: DDC 641.6 [B]--dc23
LC record available at http://lccn.loc.gov/2016962854

Contents

Early Beginnings. 4

Young Entrepreneur 6

A Small Start 8

Quick Chicken 10

Making a Name 12

Shopping Around. 14

Success & Growth. 16

Four Tenets 18

Giving Back 20

Branching Out. 22

New Roles 24

Cathy's Legacy 26

Timeline 28

Crazy Cows 29

Glossary 30

Websites. 31

Index. 32

Early Beginnings

When you are hungry for chicken, Chick-fil-A likely comes to mind. The popular food chain is known for its juicy chicken sandwiches. In fact, it was the first quick-service restaurant to serve fried chicken breast sandwiches. Founder S. Truett Cathy spent years getting the recipe just right. When he did, he knew he had something special. Americans agreed!

It was not long before Cathy's business grew from a tiny restaurant in Georgia to a nationwide chain. But Cathy was known for more than just his chicken. He was a smart businessman and **marketer**. He had a strong religious faith and gave much time and money to helping others. All these things led to Cathy's success in business and in life.

Samuel Truett Cathy was born on March 14, 1921, in Eatonton, Georgia. His parents were Lilla and Joseph. Samuel's father had been a successful farmer until beetles ruined his crops. No longer able to farm, Joseph took a job selling insurance. When Samuel was three years old, his family moved to Atlanta, Georgia, for his father's work.

Samuel had four sisters and two brothers. The family could barely survive on his father's earnings. To help pay the bills, the Cathys took in renters. Times were tough, but the family worked together to get by.

The Chick-fil-A chain has sold more than 3 billion sandwiches since its opening in 1967.

Young Entrepreneur

Samuel looked for a way to help support his family. By age eight, his work **ethic** had taken shape. Samuel bought six glass bottles of popular soft drink Coca-Cola for 25 cents total. Then he sold the bottles door-to-door for 5 cents each.

Samuel earned 30 cents total, or a profit of 5 cents, selling the six bottles of Coca-Cola. Customers were willing to pay above store price for the convenience of the beverage being delivered to their doors. Samuel's idea was so popular that he set up a drink stand in his parent's yard to help raise money for his family.

Soft drinks were just the beginning of Samuel's budding business plans. Soon, he started selling magazines door-to-door too. At age 12, he took on a newspaper route delivering the *Atlanta Journal*. Samuel delivered newspapers for several years. He was very good at signing up new readers. He learned a lot about business from this job.

As a teenager, Samuel attended Boys High School in Atlanta. After graduating in 1939, he began working for the United States **Civil Service**. He was **drafted** into the army but came down

Atlanta has grown significantly since Samuel's school days.
As of 2016, it was home to more than 30 Chick-fil-A locations!

with allergies just before his unit shipped out to the South Pacific.
Samuel's allergies kept him from joining his unit, and he was
honorably **discharged** in 1945. The same year, Samuel's brother
Ben was discharged as well. The two men decided to start working
together.

A Small Start

The Cathy brothers decided to build a restaurant. Each had saved money from previous jobs. They also took out a bank loan. The brothers used the money to buy a plot of land in Hapeville, Georgia.

Paying construction workers was expensive, so Cathy and his brother built much of the restaurant themselves. In May 1946, the doors of the Dwarf Grill opened. The restaurant fit just four tables and ten stools. It was busy with customers on opening day.

The Dwarf Grill was open every day except Sunday. The Cathy brothers were devoted Christians. They took one day a week to go to church and spend time with their families.

Cathy married Jeannette McNeil on September 19, 1948. Jeannette supported her husband's business dreams. She even began working with him.

The next year, things took a downward turn when Ben died in a plane crash. Ben's wife got his **shares** in the restaurant. She sold them to Cathy a year later. Cathy was now the sole owner.

Today, Cathy's original restaurant in Hapeville is a Chick-fil-A. A statue of Cathy sits outside.

Quick Chicken

Even without Ben's help, the Dwarf Grill was so successful that Cathy decided to open a second restaurant. In 1951, the Dwarf House opened in Forest Park, Georgia. The Dwarf Grill was renamed to match the new restaurant so customers would associate the two.

For several years, Cathy enjoyed the success of his **thriving** restaurants. Then, in 1960, the Dwarf House in Forest Park burned down. Cathy rebuilt a new restaurant on the site. But it was different. Cathy noticed self-serve, fast-service restaurants were becoming popular. He based the new restaurant on this model.

Many Forest Park diners did not like this new type of service. Cathy discussed this with another restaurant owner, Ted Davis. Davis suggested changes Cathy could make to boost the restaurant's popularity in the area. One suggestion was opening on Sundays. But Cathy did not want to work Sundays. He leased the new restaurant to Davis, and focused on his Hapeville location.

Around this time, Cathy began to experiment with a fresh idea that would set his restaurant apart. As a child, he loved his mother's fried chicken recipe, which was tasty and juicy. Cathy wanted to add this chicken to his menu. He also wanted to find a way to prepare this dish quickly. At the time, there was no fast way to cook chicken. Cathy's customers wanted a quick meal. Many worked nearby and did not have time to wait around for chicken to fry.

Cathy spent much time in the kitchen of his new restaurant, working on new recipes.

Making a Name

Cathy began working on new ways to cook chicken. He bought leftover boneless, skinless chicken breasts from Goode Brothers **Poultry**. The company made meals served on airplane flights, and sometimes the chicken was too big for the trays. The company sold the extra pieces to Cathy for a low price. Cathy experimented with cooking these chicken breasts in a new, top-secret way.

At first, Cathy put the chicken in a pan with a lid on top. The meat cooked quickly, but not quickly enough for Cathy. Then Cathy came across a gadget called a **pressure fryer**. It cooked chicken in just four minutes! The pressure fryer was exactly what Cathy needed.

Chick-fil-A still serves all-natural chicken breast meat. The chicken is breaded by hand daily in the restaurants.

The original Chick-fil-A sandwich was served on a buttered, toasted bun and with a side of dill pickle chips.

Cathy did not only want his chicken to cook fast. He wanted it to taste good too. He spent several years testing variations of the recipe on his customers.

Finally, Cathy got it right. He kept his recipe top secret, but he knew it was ready to serve to his customers. The dish was the first fried, boneless, skinless chicken breast sandwich sold in a US restaurant.

Chick-fil-A was the name for Cathy's **signature** menu item. He used the best parts of a chicken to make his sandwich. *Fillet* (fih-LAY) is a term for a boneless cut of meat. Cathy decided to call his dish chicken fillet, but spelled Chick-fil-A. The capital *A* represented the fact that people were getting a top-quality product.

Shopping Around

Cathy **trademarked** the name Chick-fil-A in 1963. This meant no other restaurants could name their chicken dishes the same. But Cathy did want his competitors to serve Chick-fil-A. He turned his recipe into a product they could buy and add to their menu. Cathy packaged premade breading that was ready to cook. Within four months, 50 restaurants signed up to buy it.

Over the next few years, Cathy told as many people as he could about his Chick-fil-A breading. He wanted Chick-fil-A to be served in more places. But he also had concerns that other restaurants were not cooking the recipe to his quality. Cathy began to worry about tying the Chick-fil-A name to poor-quality products. He decided he needed to make the sandwiches himself if he wanted them done right.

Cathy's Chick-fil-A was still sold at the Dwarf House, which remained a popular restaurant. But Cathy wanted to open a second place where people could eat his famous sandwich. He knew building another restaurant would be expensive. So, he decided to try something different. He paid to rent a shop in Greenbriar Mall in

The original Chick-fil-A restaurant is still open today in the Greenbriar Mall. It bears a sign describing the site's history.

Atlanta. This way, Cathy did not have to pay for land or construction of a new building. In 1967, the first Chick-fil-A restaurant opened at the mall. At the time, there were very few restaurants in malls.

Success & Growth

The Chick-fil-A restaurant was a huge success. It was Greenbriar Mall's only restaurant. Hungry shoppers no longer had to leave the mall to find a meal. Cathy decided to open other restaurants using the same **strategy**.

It was around this time that a man named Jimmy Collins officially joined the Chick-fil-A team. Collins was a kitchen designer. Cathy had worked with Collins to design the Dwarf House and the first Chick-fil-A restaurants.

Collins knew the restaurant business and was a devoted Christian like Cathy. These **traits** made Cathy trust him. So, when Cathy was looking for someone to help open new stores, he asked Collins to help. In 1968, Collins agreed to come onboard as vice president of Chick-fil-A company.

Over the next few years, the men worked together to open new Chick-fil-A locations in malls across the South. By 1971, there were seven Chick-fil-As across Georgia, North Carolina, and South Carolina. But Cathy and Collins weren't done. Just three years later, that number tripled.

As the company grew, Cathy knew he needed to put standards in place for his teams. He thought a lot about how he wanted to run his business. Cathy started to shape the Chick-fil-A business philosophy.

Cathy behind the counter of his original restaurant in 2001. He continued to visit all locations as his company expanded.

Four Tenets

Cathy's Christian faith was important to him. He believed in treating others well. He also had high standards. Cathy wanted to **incorporate** these concepts into his business. In 1971, he came up with four **tenets** for Chick-fil-A.

First, Cathy selected an operator for each new location. The operator invested a small amount of money to help get the restaurant set up. He or she would then attend special training to learn Cathy's high quality standards. After the training, the operators ran their own locations, receiving a salary and a portion of the restaurant's profits.

Second, Cathy decided to open Chick-fil-As only in shopping malls. Malls were becoming very popular. There was great opportunity for fast growth without construction or many start-up costs.

Third, Cathy wanted to keep control over the business. He used the profits from his other locations to build new restaurants. This was a slower process than taking out bank loans to set up new locations. But Cathy felt the extra wait was worth it to avoid loan **debt**.

Cathy's faith played a role in Chick-fil-As being closed Sundays.
Sunday is a day of worship in the Christian faith.

Fourth, Cathy made his employees his top **priority**. He wanted them to enjoy going to work. He also wanted them to have time with their family and friends. For this reason, Chick-fil-As were closed every Sunday. This gave employees a day of rest. Another day of business could have made Cathy a lot of money. But he put the well-being of his employees ahead of his business.

Giving Back

Treating his employees well remained important to Cathy. In 1973, he started a college **scholarship** program for them. The Team Member Scholarship program was for Chick-fil-A employees who wanted to go to college but may not have been able to afford it.

In its first year, Cathy gave out a $1,000 scholarship to one employee. Over the years, he added more money to the scholarship fund. Soon, he was able to give more employees scholarships. Chick-fil-A has given over $30 million to more than 30,000 team members since it began its scholarship program.

The scholarship program was not the only way Cathy gave back to his employees. In 1975, he started a program called Symbol of Success. Each year, Chick-fil-A awards the top restaurant operators a new car. The company has given away more than 1,000 cars through this program.

Keeping customers happy was equally important to Cathy. At his first restaurant, which was open 24 hours a day, he once worked a 36-hour shift! There were no other employees available to do the job, and Cathy did not want to disappoint his diners.

In 2008, President George W. Bush (left) gave Cathy the President's Volunteer Service Award.

Branching Out

By 1984, Chick-fil-A had been very successful for many years. That year, it established headquarters in Atlanta. This cost $10 million! The cost of chicken breasts was also rising. This meant Chick-fil-A made less profit.

In addition, Chick-fil-A now had competition. Other restaurants were moving into malls, meaning shoppers now had a choice of where to eat. These shoppers did not always choose Chick-fil-A. This led to company sales falling.

Cathy looked to his company's leaders to help him find new ways to bring in money. They began to talk about why they were in business. Over time, their talks began to center on their religious beliefs. Together, the leaders decided to make this the focus of a new company purpose.

Chick-fil-A leaders led positive lifestyles and treated people well. They believed these actions would rub off on their employees, which would result in an excellent experience for Chick-fil-A customers. Their plan worked. Within a year, sales rose by more than 36 percent.

Today, the WinShape Foundation has overnight and day camps in 15 states.

Cathy also encouraged his team to give back to the community. As part of this philosophy, he started the WinShape Foundation in 1984. It was built on the idea of shaping winners. Cathy wanted to build strong future leaders through meaningful experiences. The foundation funded a variety of projects in the coming years, including a kids' summer camp in 1985.

New Roles

By the mid-1980s, Chick-fil-A had increased sales, and Cathy's additional programs were flourishing. But, there was still the problem of mall restaurant competition. Cathy rethought his **tenet** that Chick-fil-As were to be located only in malls. He opened the first free-standing Chick-fil-A in 1986, in Atlanta.

Two years later, Cathy made another big change. He passed the role of president to Collins, and became instead the company's chairman of the board and chief executive officer. One year later, Cathy took on another new role. He wrote the first of his six books, *It's Easier to Succeed than to Fail.*

In 1992, he expanded the locations of his Chick-fil-As. These included on college campuses and in supermarkets, medical centers, and airports. The restaurant chain was more successful than ever.

Cathy's success had a lot to do with how he **marketed** his restaurants. The company's most famous marketing idea came in 1995. Chick-fil-A began using talking cows in its ads. These cows urged people to eat chicken instead of beef. The ads were comical, and a hit with many customers.

The Chick-fil-A cows have appeared at many events. In 2015, some were given names! These include Freedom, Freckles, Kat, and Molly.

Cathy's Legacy

In 1996, Cathy celebrated 50 years in the restaurant business by opening a 1950s-themed diner called Truett's Grill. The first diner was located in Morrow, Georgia. Today, there are three Truett's Grill locations in Georgia.

In 2000, Cathy reached another milestone. The company made $1 billion in sales. A year later, Chick-fil-A opened its one-thousandth store. Over the next decade, Cathy's business continued to grow. In 2013, Truett's Luau opened in Fayetteville, Georgia. It offered fresh seafood as well as popular Chick-fil-A menu items.

The following year, Cathy died at the age of 93. At the time, there were more than 1,800 Chick-fil-As across the country. The company continues to expand today.

Cathy's **legacy** lives on in his three children and 19 grandchildren. Before his death, he made his family promise to never sell **shares** in the company. He wanted them to carry on his vision for Chick-fil-A.

Today, Cathy's son Dan is the company's CEO, chairman, and president. Cathy's other son, Don, is the executive vice president.

Chick-fil-A

BREAKFAST
IN LOVING MEMORY
TRUETT CATHY
1921 - 2014
CLOSED SUNDAY

Several Chick-fil-A locations paid tribute to Cathy in the days and weeks following his death.

Their sister, Trudy, is the director of WinShape Camps for Girls. Some of Cathy's grandchildren now work for Chick-fil-A too. It seems certain the family tradition of quality chicken will continue far into the future.

Timeline

1921 — Samuel Truett Cathy was born on March 14, in Eatonton, Georgia.

1946 — In May, Cathy and his brother Ben opened the doors to the Dwarf Grill.

1963 — Cathy trademarked the Chick-fil-A name.

1967 — Cathy opened the first Chick-fil-A in Greenbriar Mall in Atlanta, Georgia.

1971 — Cathy came up with his four tenets for running the Chick-fil-A business.

1986 — The first free-standing Chick-fil-A opened in Atlanta.

1992 — Cathy started putting restaurants in locations such as college campuses, supermarkets, medical centers, and airports.

1996 — Cathy opened the first Truett's Grill.

2001 — Chick-fil-A opened its one-thousandth store.

2014 — On September 8, Cathy died at the age of 93.

Crazy Cows

Have you ever seen a cow with a paintbrush? In 1995, a billboard advertising Chick-fil-A in Georgia featured just that. A cow stood on the back of another cow, held a paintbrush in its mouth, and wrote the words "Eat Mor Chikin" on the sign. People thought the ad was funny. If you eat more chicken, it means you will likely eat fewer cows.

Soon, the cows started to appear in Chick-fil-A TV ads. The ads were very popular. Chick-fil-A used the cows in ads for many years.

1995: The Chick-fil-A cows appeared on their first billboard.

1997: Chick-fil-A made its first commercial featuring the cows.

2002: The website eatmorchikin.com launched.

2006: A 3-D Chick-fil-A cow held a sign at a baseball game.

2008: A 3-D Chick-fil-A cow hung from a water tower painted with the famous words "Eat Mor Chikin."

2017: The cows had more than 690,000 followers on Facebook.

Glossary

civil service - the part of the government that is responsible for matters not covered by the military, the courts, or the law.

debt (DEHT) - something owed to someone, especially money.

discharge - to release from military service.

draft - to select for required military service.

ethic - a theory or set of moral values held by an individual.

incorporate - to include something as part of another thing.

legacy - something important or meaningful handed down from previous generations or from the past.

market - to advertise or promote an item for sale. A person who performs these tasks is a marketer.

poultry - farm birds raised for their eggs and meat. Chickens, turkeys, ducks, and geese are poultry.

pressure fryer - a device that cooks meat quickly using pressure and cooking oil brought to high temperatures.

priority - the condition of coming before others, as in order or importance.

scholarship - money awarded to a person to help pay for that person's schooling.

share - one of the equal parts into which the ownership of a
   company is divided.
signature - something that sets apart or identifies an individual,
   group, or company.
strategy - a careful plan or method.
tenet - a principle or belief important to an individual or to a group.
thrive - to do well.
trademark - to register a word or feature that identifies a certain
   company. Something that is trademarked cannot be used by
   others without permission.
trait - a quality or feature of something.

Websites

To learn more about Food Dudes,
visit **abdobooklinks.com**. These links are routinely monitored
and updated to provide the most current information available.

Index

A
allergies 7
army 6, 7
Atlanta Journal 6

B
birth 4
books 24

C
Cathy, Ben 5, 7, 8, 10
Cathy, Dan 26
Cathy, Don 26
Cathy, Joseph 4, 5
Cathy, Lilla 4, 10
Cathy White, Trudy 27
Chick-fil-A breading 14
Chick-fil-A cows 24
Chick-fil-A name 13, 14
Chick-fil-A tenets 17, 18, 19, 24
chicken recipes 4, 11, 12, 13, 14
chicken sandwiches 4, 13, 14
childhood jobs 6
Collins, Jimmy 16, 24

D
Davis, Ted 10
death 26
Dwarf Grill 8, 10
Dwarf House 10, 14, 16

E
education 6

F
family 4, 5, 6, 7, 8, 10, 19, 26, 27

G
Georgia 4, 6, 8, 10, 15, 16, 22, 24, 26
  Atlanta 4, 6, 15, 22, 24
  Eatonton 4
  Fayetteville 26
  Forest Park 10
  Hapeville 8, 10
  Morrow 26
Goode Brothers Poultry 12
Greenbriar Mall 14, 15, 16

M
marriage 8
McNeil, Jeannette 8

N
North Carolina 16

P
pressure fryer 12

R
religious faith 4, 8, 16, 18, 22

S
South Carolina 16
Sunday, closed on 8, 10, 19
Symbol of Success 20

T
Team Member Scholarship 20
Truett's Grill 26
Truett's Luau 26

U
United States Civil Service 6

W
WinShape Foundation 23, 27